Y0-AGJ-703

I CAN BE A
FOOTBALL PLAYER

By Carol Greene

Prepared under the direction of Robert Hillerich, Ph.D.

 CHILDRENS PRESS ™

CHICAGO

Library of Congress Cataloging in Publication Data

Greene, Carol.
  I can be a football player.

  Summary: Discusses the life of a football player,
a job which is lucrative, but hard work, too.
  1. Football—Juvenile literature. 2. Football
players—Juvenile literature. [1. Football players.
2. Occupations] I. Title. II. Title: Football
player.
GV950.7.G74   1984   796.332   84-9609
ISBN 0-516-01839-6

With special thanks to Coach Dale Collier

PICTURE DICTIONARY

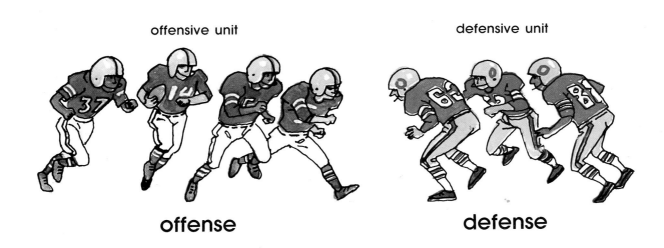

offensive unit

defensive unit

offense

defense

positions ➡

running back

quarterback

running back

wing back

right end

right tackle

right guard

center

left guard

left tackle

tight end

team

coach

practice

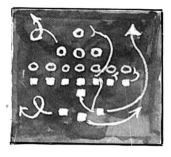

play

announcer

fans

referee

score

touchdown

money

pro

professional

training camp

season

charities

Football players who play for money are called professionals.

What is a football
player? That's easy. A
football player is
someone who plays
football.

money

professional

Some football players
play for fun. Other
football players play for
fun and money. They are
called professionals.

Center is ready to snap the ball to the quarterback

team

Football players play on a team. Each team is divided into two parts or units. Each unit uses eleven players.

One unit plays when the team has the ball. Its players try to score. It is

called the offensive unit.
The other unit plays when
the team does not have
the ball. Its players try to
stop the other team from
scoring. It is called the
defensive unit.

offensive unit   defensive unit

Today most professional football players are men. But women play football, too. These women (below) play for the Detroit Fillies.

·Number 14, the quarterback, has just thrown the football to a teammate.

Each player has a special job. But all players must work together, too. They must be a team.

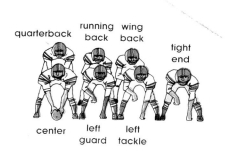

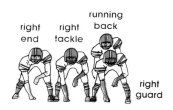

positions
(special
job)

Football players must be strong. At training camp they practice blocking (above).
They do stretching exercises (below) to keep their muscles from tightening up.

Professional football players go to training camp each year for about two months. There they work six days a week.

training camp

Part of the time they work in classrooms. They study the plays or moves that other teams use. They study plays that they will use.

plays

But most of the time, players work outside at training camp. They exercise and jog. They practice the plays they have studied.

coach

practice

Coaches show players how to do their special jobs better. The head coach helps everyone work together.

Dave Williams, number 22 (above), carries the ball over
the top to make the first down. Players who carry the
ball must be strong and fast.

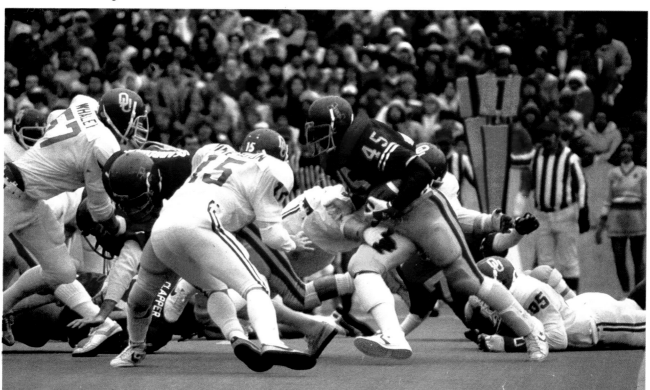

Near the end of training camp, the team plays with other teams. Then they find out how good they really are.

Professional teams play about sixteen games during the football

season

season. About half are in their home city. About half are in other cities.

Defensive ends, numbers 73 and 82, (above) try to rush the quarterback,
number 12. A fullback, number 39, (below) runs up the middle.

Winning teams may play extra games—such as the Super Bowl. They earn extra money for these games—even if they lose.

Professional football players do not work about four months each year. They can spend this time with their families and friends.

18

Some work for charities, such as the Red Cross. Some help children learn to play football. Some make money by being in movies or TV ads. Others write books.

charities

Running back (top), middle line-
backer (above left), and running
back Walter Payton (right)

Professional football players must be strong and fast. They must always stay in good shape.

Players must get along well with other people, too. They must like hard work. And they must want to win.

Football is a hard game. Players must
:   be mentally and physically strong.

Some people think
football players don't
have to be smart. That's
wrong. Football players
must be able to think
fast. One little mistake
can lose a game.

Thousands of fans watch the marching band perform before the start of the game at Michigan State University.

Most football players go to college. They study other things and play football, too. Professional teams hire them after college.

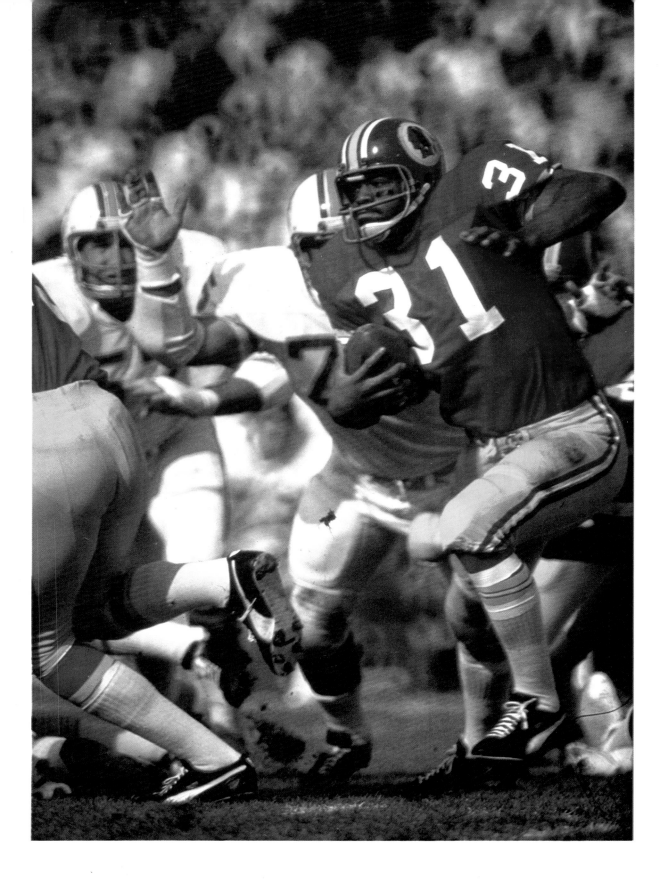

Football players usually play on professional teams for about five years. Then they find other jobs.

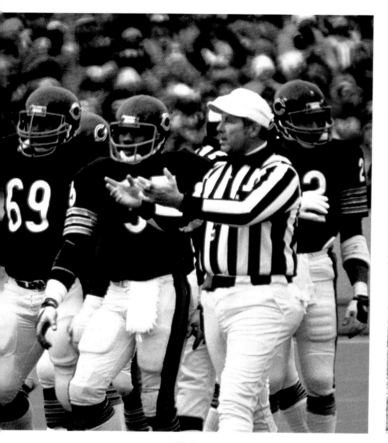

Referee

Coach

referee

Some become
teachers or coaches or
referees. Some write
about sports for
newspapers. Some

Football players model fur coats
at a charity fashion show (above).
Johnny Morris, a former player,
has become a TV sports announcer.

become announcers for
radio or TV. Some go into
different fields. They might
sell things or open a
restaurant.

announcer

Football players work
hard. But they think it's
worth it—especially when
they hear the fans
cheering for them.

WORDS YOU SHOULD KNOW

announcer (uh • NOWN • ser)—a person who talks about a game or gives the news on radio or TV

charity (CHARE • ih • tee)—a group that helps the poor, the sick, or others who need help

cheer (CHEER)—to yell for the one you want to win

classroom (KLAS • room)—the room where people come together to learn

coach (KOHCH)—someone who teaches and trains a team or a person to do something

college (KAHL • ij)—a school for higher learning. It follows high school.

defensive (di • FEN • siv) **unit**—those who try to keep the other team from making points

divide (dih • VIDE)—to break into parts

especially (e • SPESH • ih • lee)—chiefly or more than other times

exercise (EK • ser • syz)—working out the body

extra (EK • struh)—more than is usual

fan (FAN)—a person who really cares a lot about something

football (FOOT • bawl)—a game played by two teams with eleven people each on a large field that has a goal at each end

hire (HYR)—to give a job for pay

jog (JAHG)—to run or trot slowly

movie (MOO • vee)—a moving picture that tells a story

newspaper (NOOZ • pay • per or NYOOZ • pay • per) —a paper that has news, ads, stories, pictures, and other things people will want to read

offensive (uh • FEN • siv) **unit**—those who try to make points in a game

player (PLAY • er)—someone or something that plays

professional (pruh • FESH • ih • nil)—a person who does for pay what some people do only for fun

referee (ref • ih • REE)—a person who decides about plays in certain sports and games

score (SKOR)—the record of the number of points made in a contest or game or on a test

someone (SUM • wun)—some person

sport (SPORT)—a game or contest

study (STUD • ee)—to try to learn by reading and thinking

unit (YOO • nit)—any group of people or things that are thought of as one whole part

write (RYTE)—to put down in letters and words

INDEX

PHOTO CREDITS

Nawrocki Stock Photo:
  © Jim Whitmer—4 (top)
  © Candee Productions—cover, 6
  © Carlos Vergara—12 (top)
  © Schulman—20 (top)
  © Jim Wright—22 (left), 28 (top), 29 (left)
  © M.J. Lepczyk—23

Hillstrom Stock Photos:
  © Carl Sissac—4 (bottom), 8 (top), 10 (top), 14 (top), 16 (top), 18,
    20 (bottom right), 26 (left), 27 (2 photos), 28 (bottom)
  © Donald C. Johnson—29 (right)

EKM—Nepenthe:
  © Robert Ginn—12 (bottom)

© Laurel Spingola—7, 26 (right)

© Stock Boston, Inc./Photographer J. Berndt—8 (bottom), 22 (right)

Stock Boston:
  © Tim Carlson—9, 16 (bottom)
  © Cary Wolinsky—10 (bottom)
  © Bill Gillette—14 (bottom)

A Stock:
  © Dave Maenze—20 (bottom left), 24

ABOUT THE AUTHOR

Carol Greene has written over 40 books for children, plus stories, poems, songs, and filmstrips. She has also worked as a children's editor and a teacher of writing for children. She received a B.A. in English Literature from Park College, Parkville, Missouri, and an M.A. in Musicology from Indiana University. Ms. Greene lives in St. Louis, Missouri. When she isn't writing she likes to read, travel, sing, do volunteer work at her church—and write some more.

DATE DUE

MAY 1	OCT. 21		
NOV 5			
SEP 18			
OCT 14			
OCT 21			
OCT 28			
NOV 11			
NOV 24			
JAN 13			
JAN 20			
APR 12			
OCT 5			